STECK-VAUGHN

PORTRAIT OF AMERICA

Steck-Vaughn Company

Executive Editor	Diane Sharpe
Senior Editor	Martin S. Saiewitz
Design Manager	Pamela Heaney
Photo Editor	Margie Foster
Electronic Cover Graphics	Alan Klemp

Proof Positive/Farrowlyne Associates, Inc.
Program Editorial, Revision Development, Design, and Production

Consultant: Kenneth Feld, Vermont Department of Travel & Tourism

Published by Raintree Steck-Vaughn Publishers, an imprint of Steck-Vaughn Company.

A Turner Educational Services, Inc. book. Based on the Portrait of America television series by R. E. (Ted) Turner.

Cover Photo: Stowe, Vermont, by © Peter Miller/The Image Bank.

Library of Congress Cataloging-in-Publication Data

Thompson, Kathleen.
    Vermont / Kathleen Thompson.
      p. cm. — (Portrait of America)
    "Based on the Portrait of America television series" — T.p. verso.
    "A Turner book."
    Includes index.
    ISBN 0-8114-7391-0 (library binding). — ISBN 0-8114-7472-0 (softcover)
    1. Vermont—Juvenile literature. [1. Vermont.] I. Portrait of
America (Television program) II. Title. III. Series. IV. Series:
Thompson, Kathleen. Portrait of America.
F49.3.T48 1996
974.3—dc20
                                           95-50027
                                         CIP
                                         AC

Printed and Bound in the United States of America

4 5 6 7 8 9 10 WZ 03 02 01 00

Acknowledgments
The publishers wish to thank the following for permission to reproduce photographs:
Pp. 7, 8 © Superstock; p. 10 Charles A. Parant III; p. 11 National Life Insurance Company, Montpelier; p. 12 Vermont Historical Society; p. 14 National Life Insurance Company, Montpelier; p. 15 (both) Vermont Historical Society; p. 16 National Portrait Gallery, Smithsonian Institution; p. 17 Vermont Historical Society; p. 19 UPI/Bettmann; p. 20 Old Stone House Museum; p. 21 © Glen Barber/Old Stone House Museum; p. 22 IBM; p. 24 (top) IBM, (bottom) Vermont Marble Company; pp. 25, 26 (both) Vermont Department of Travel & Tourism; p. 27 (top) Vermont Department of Agriculture, (bottom) © Superstock; pp. 28, 29 (both), 30, 31 Ben & Jerry's; p. 32 Vermont Department of Travel & Tourism; p. 34 © Erik Borg; p. 36 (top) Vermont Fish & Wildlife, (bottom) Vermont Department of Travel & Tourism; p. 37 Architect of the Capitol; pp. 38, 39 (both) © Clemens Kalischer; pp. 40, 41 © Paul O. Boisvert; p. 42 © Michael Reagan; p. 44 Vermont Fish & Wildlife; p. 46 One Mile Up; p. 47 (left) One Mile Up, (center, right) Vermont Department of Travel & Tourism.

STECK-VAUGHN

PORTRAIT OF AMERICA

Vermont

Kathleen Thompson

A Turner Book

RSVP

RAINTREE
STECK-VAUGHN
PUBLISHERS

The Steck-Vaughn Company

Austin, Texas

Vermont

North Troy

Newport

Saint Albans

▲ Mount Mansfield

Burlington

St. Johnsbury

Waterbury

Lake
Champlain

MONTPELIER ✪

Bristol

GREEN
MOUNTAIN
NATIONAL STATE
FOREST

Barre

Middlebury

MOUNTAINS

White River

Rutland

Woodstock

Plymouth

GREEN
MOUNTAIN
NATIONAL STATE
FOREST

Springfield

Connecticut River

Arlington

GREEN

Bellows Falls

Brattleboro

Bennington

Contents

Introduction

Vermont is a New England state of unspoiled beauty. Three fourths of the state is covered with rich forestland. There are 430 lakes and ponds. The scenic Green Mountains run the length of the state, dividing east from west. Many of the people of Vermont live off the land and have worked hard to care for it. Their love of rural living has spurred Vermont citizens to write some of the strictest environmental protection laws in the nation. These laws limit major developments that would damage lands, rivers, lakes, and air. The people of Vermont make sacrifices for what they believe in. And what they believe in most is a beautiful land called Vermont!

Vermont produces more maple syrup than any other state. When maple sap is collected, it is taken to a sugar house, such as this one in Waterford. There, it is boiled down into syrup or sugar.

Vermont

The Green Mountain State

In the fifteenth century, the Vermont area was inhabited by Native American people called the Algonquins. The Algonquins were divided into many smaller groups living throughout the region now known as New England. The Algonquin groups who lived in present-day Vermont were the Abenaki, the Pennacook, and the Mahican.

These groups had similar lifestyles. They had turned much of the area into a communal hunting ground, where they hunted deer, bears, and small game. Some also grew corn, squash, and other vegetables. They made canoes out of birch bark for fishing and travel. Their houses were also made mostly of birch bark.

Around 1500 the Iroquois League, a federation of several other Native American groups, battled the Abenaki, Mahican, and Pennacook people. They took over much of the Vermont hunting ground and drove many of the Algonquins out of the area. Those who stayed had to live under the rule of the Iroquois.

Collecting maple sap for making maple syrup or maple sugar was first done by Native Americans. Early explorers wrote about the "sweet water" Native Americans drew from trees.

French explorer Samuel de Champlain and his party arrived in the Vermont area in 1609. Champlain traveled south from Canada as far as Vermont's Green Mountains. There Champlain made friends with the Algonquins and helped them defeat the Iroquois and drive them out of the area.

In return for Champlain's help, the Algonquins, especially the Abenaki, helped him explore the Vermont area. Champlain mapped the region and claimed it for France. He also named a lake there after himself. Champlain and the French explorers who came after him admired the lush green mountains of the area. The name Vermont grew out of these descriptions, combining the French words *vert* and *mont*, which mean "green" and "mountain."

Throughout the 1600s, the French set up fur-trading posts and forts in the Vermont area, but did not try to establish any permanent settlements. To the south and the east of the area, settlers from England were establishing 13 colonies. Present-day Vermont was included as part of the Massachusetts Colony. The settlers were uneasy with the amount of land the French occupied west of the 13 colonies. In about 1690 a series

These rock drawings were left by the Pennacook at Bellows Falls, on the Connecticut River.

of battles between the French and English settlers began in the area of present-day Canada. The battles soon spread along the western edge of the colonies as far south as present-day South Carolina.

French explorer Samuel de Champlain was probably the first European to see the Vermont area. He arrived there in 1609.

To protect its settlements from the French, the Massachusetts Colony erected a series of forts along the Connecticut River. Fort Dummer was established in 1724 near the present-day city of Brattleboro, Vermont. It was the area's first permanent British settlement. The Dutch also established a settlement called Pownal to the west of Fort Dummer that same year.

The dispute over land led to war between the French and the British. The war is known as the French and Indian War because many Native American groups fought alongside the French. Some Native American groups also fought with the British, however. In 1763 the French and Indian War ended, and France surrendered nearly all of North America east of the Mississippi River to Great Britain.

The French defeat did not end all land disputes in the area, however. Some ongoing boundary disagreements between colonies still were not settled. In 1741 British King George II took away Massachusetts's northern claims and set its northern boundary at its present location. In 1749 Governor Benning Wentworth of New Hampshire claimed the lands west of the Connecticut River as far as the Hudson River. Today the Connecticut River forms the eastern boundary of Vermont. The settlements on this land were called the New Hampshire Grants. New York's governor George Clinton, however, believed his land extended east from the Hudson River to the Connecticut River. King George III tried to settle the dispute in 1764 by declaring that the property belonged to New York. He ordered the people living on the New Hampshire Grants to either leave or pay New York for the land.

However, the New Hampshire Grants settlers didn't think that King George's decree was fair. They ignored it and stayed on their land. The government of New York tried to force the settlers already in Vermont to buy new titles for their land. The Vermonters refused. Instead they formed a militia to defend themselves. The Green Mountain Boys, as they called themselves, succeeded in keeping the New Yorkers out of the disputed area. In a few years, everyone's attention turned to a larger battle—the battle for American independence.

By 1775 the 13 American colonies believed they were ready to rule themselves. They protested British laws and staged public demonstrations. In April 1775 shots were fired at Lexington and Concord in Massachusetts, and the Revolutionary War began.

One month after the start of

This drawing shows Ethan Allen and the Green Mountain Boys capturing Fort Ticonderoga. Many historians call the capture the first offensive action taken by the colonists in the Revolutionary War.

TI·CON·DER·OGA

Ethan Allen a
Fort Ticondero
May 10th 177

the war, about two hundred Green Mountain Boys and other volunteers captured the British Fort Ticonderoga, which was on the New York side of Lake Champlain. They dislodged the cannons and dragged them all the way to Boston. In 1776, George Washington used the cannons to help drive the British out of Boston. As the war went on, the Green Mountain Boys also helped defeat the British in many other battles, especially the Battle of Bennington in 1777.

As sympathetic as the Green Mountain Boys were to the colonists' cause, they didn't want to join the United States. They wanted to form their own country instead. At the start of 1777, settlers in the disputed area—then called New Connecticut—formed an independent republic. The constitution of this new republic was the first in the country to outlaw slavery and to allow all adult males, regardless of how much money and property they had, to vote.

When the Americans won the Revolutionary War in 1783, New Connecticut was still an independent republic. Both New York and New Hampshire believed that they still had rights to the land, however. Finally, in 1790, New York and New Hampshire gave up their claims. With these disputes settled, Vermont voted to join the United States. It became the fourteenth state in March 1791.

Vermont developed a profitable trade with its British neighbors in Canada. But as the United States expanded its worldwide trade, Great Britain became increasingly hostile. The British didn't welcome the Americans competing with them for overseas trade,

When Vermont entered the Union in 1791, it was the first state to join the original 13 colonies.

so they began to attack American trading ships. The United States declared war on Great Britain in 1812.

Many Vermont citizens were against the War of 1812 because it stopped their profitable trade with the British in Canada. By the time the war ended in 1814, Vermont's economy had been seriously hurt. In 1823 the Champlain Canal connecting Lake Champlain to the Hudson River was completed. The canal made it possible for Vermont farmers to ship goods to New York City, making trade with Canada less important.

By the 1820s more and more western states were being admitted to the Union. A national debate had formed concerning the rights of new states to allow slavery. Slave labor was crucial to the farm economy of the South, but it was generally viewed as immoral by wage-paying northerners. Since Vermont had been among the first states to outlaw slavery, its residents were especially outspoken in the debate.

During the Civil War, 22 Confederate soldiers rode into St. Albans and robbed its banks.

In 1861 the disagreements between the North and the South expanded into the Civil War. About 35,000 soldiers from Vermont—more than one tenth of the state's population—served in the war. After the Union won the Civil War in 1865, millions of former slaves chose to stay in the South. Others moved to the North or joined the thousands of pioneers moving to the West.

After the Civil War, dairy farming and wood processing became important parts of Vermont's

This photograph shows workers at the Excelsior Granite Company, one of the many mining operations to thrive in Vermont after the Civil War.

15

economy. Granite, marble, and copper mining also grew in importance. The state's population was boosted when immigrants from Canada, Great Britain, Scandinavia, and Italy began arriving in Vermont about this time.

Vermont's Chester A. Arthur had served as Vice President for about four months when President James A. Garfield was shot in an attempted assassination in 1881. When Garfield died a few months later, Arthur took office as the country's twenty-first President. He served until 1884.

Just before the start of the twentieth century, Vermont added a new industry. In 1891 Vermont became the nation's first state with an office of publicity to encourage tourism. As the rest of the nation became increasingly industrialized, people began to look for vacation spots away from the bustle of the cities. By 1911, when the office of publicity expanded and officially named itself the Bureau of Publicity, new Vermont vacation resorts were already thriving.

When the United States entered World War I in 1917, Vermont donated one million dollars to the war effort. Almost twenty thousand Vermont citizens served in the armed forces. About 650 of these gave their lives to help the United States and its allies win the war.

In 1923 Calvin Coolidge of Vermont became the nation's thirtieth President and the second from the Green Mountain State. Coolidge had served as Vice President under Warren G. Harding for almost two years when Harding died in office. Because Coolidge didn't have time to get to Washington, D.C., he was

Calvin Coolidge was sworn in as the nation's thirtieth President on August 3, 1923. Later, Coolidge was asked what he first thought upon becoming President. He replied, "I thought I could swing it."

A disastrous flood struck Montpelier and other areas of Vermont in 1927. Vermont accepted federal monetary assistance for the first time to rebuild the state after the flood.

sworn in by his father in his Vermont childhood home. Coolidge was a popular President, and he was elected to serve a second term in 1924.

Things had been going well economically for Vermont for many years, but 1927 marked the beginning of difficult times. In November the state was struck by a devastating flood that killed about sixty people in two days. No neighborhood near a river escaped the waters, which drowned livestock, destroyed roads, and sometimes even carried away buildings and bridges.

Just as Vermont was beginning to recover from the floods, the huge economic slump of the 1930s, called the Great Depression, fell upon the nation. Some of the state's more isolated farmers, who were already having financial difficulties, didn't feel the effects of the slowing economy. But most of Vermont suffered as factories, mills, and farms were forced to shut down, putting many people out of work.

When Franklin D. Roosevelt took office as President of the United States in 1932, however, the economy in Vermont and across the nation began to improve. Roosevelt put unemployed people across the nation back to work building public structures such as roads, buildings, and parks. Vermont was especially aided by the construction of dams, bridges, and even ski slopes.

The Depression ended with the start of World War II. When the United States entered the war in December 1941, about twenty-five thousand Vermont citizens were in the armed services. Others found jobs in Vermont factories and mills. Some even commuted to work in Connecticut and Massachusetts when there were no more war jobs left in Vermont.

After the United States and its allies won the war in 1945, the high demand for manufactured materials dropped. Vermont realized that it needed to bring more industries into the state to keep its economy going. The Vermont Development Department, instituted in 1949, helped the state expand its manufacturing, especially the electronics industry. But in spite of all the new factories and corporations, Vermont still managed to maintain its small-town atmosphere. This helped the tourist industry continue to thrive. In the 1960s, visitors eager to participate in winter activities and sports were especially attracted to Vermont.

Not all of the newcomers to Vermont during these years were tourists. In fact, since the 1960s the state has grown by at least fifty thousand new residents every ten years. Vermont quickly realized there were drawbacks to such rapid growth. To prevent pollution and overdevelopment in the face of this rapid expansion, the Vermont legislature passed the Environmental Control Law in 1970. This law continues to give the state control over any development that threatens Vermont's environment.

With the election of Madeleine Kunin as governor in 1984, Vermont continued to make the preservation of its environment a top priority. Kunin helped pass the Growth Management Act of 1988, which gave even more environmental control of the land to the state. Kunin was an important Vermont figure in other ways, also. Besides being the first woman elected governor in Vermont's history, Kunin worked to get more women involved in the state government. By the early 1990s, Vermont had the highest percentage of women legislators in the nation.

Vermont celebrated its two hundredth birthday in 1991 and was proud to note how well it has maintained the qualities of its rural past. Not all Vermont residents think that the environment should continue to be a top priority, however. Many believe that the state should concentrate on economic development, to ensure a secure financial future. As the twenty-first century approaches, Vermont residents are working to resolve this issue in a way that benefits both the economy and the environment.

Madeleine Kunin, governor of Vermont from 1985 to 1991, addresses the 1988 Democratic National Convention.

A Self-Made Man

Imagine what it would be like to grow up without going to school. People would have to learn how to read and write by themselves. That's what Alexander Lucius Twilight did. For Twilight, born in 1795, it was even harder to educate himself than it might be for people today. His struggle for an education provided the opportunity to attend school to many young people who might not have attended otherwise.

Tradition has it that Alexander Twilight became an indentured servant when he was eight years old. Indentured servitude meant that a person would borrow money and then work for a certain amount of time to pay it back. Twilight was supposed to work on a farm for 15 years. Somehow, during this time he managed to teach himself to read. Meanwhile, he also saved enough money to buy back his last year of servitude.

When Twilight was about twenty years old, he enrolled in a grammar school called Randolph Academy.

Twilight graduated from Randolph Academy in six years. Two years later, he graduated from Middlebury College.

Middlebury claims Twilight as the first African American to graduate from a United States college. Twilight's race is sometimes debated by historians, although some of Twilight's ancestors were probably African American. The Twilight family was sometimes classified as African American and sometimes as European American

This is the only photo ever taken of Alexander Twilight.

Alexander Twilight named the school he built "Athenian Hall," but people in Orleans County called it the "Stone House." Now the building is called the Old Stone House Museum.

in census polls. Whatever Twilight's ancestry, however, his accomplishments are clear.

In 1829 Alexander Twilight became the principal at Brownington Academy, the Orleans County grammar school. He managed the school aggressively, increasing enrollment by advertising for students from other towns. Enrollment increased so much there was not enough room for all the students. Twilight then built a large granite school and dormitory. He also paid for the new school, since the school board refused to approve it.

When the school was completed, Twilight was elected to the Vermont legislature. He was probably the first African American to serve in a state legislature. He asked the legislators to continue funding Brownington, instead of splitting the money with another school, but they refused. Twilight then returned to teaching.

Alexander Twilight died in 1857. The old school still stands as a monument to a man who believed that every young person deserves a good education.

An Effective Workforce

Many people think of cows and dairy products when asked to comment on the economy of Vermont. They're partly right—agriculture is still important in Vermont. But the ingredients that make up the state's economy are much more varied than many people might think.

Manufacturing is still important to Vermont's economy. The character of the state's factories and industries differs from most states, however. For one thing, there are very few large companies in Vermont. In fact, most manufacturing companies have fewer than 150 employees. Even so, manufacturing contributes about $2.3 billion each year to Vermont's economy.

The most important area of manufacturing in Vermont is electrical machinery and equipment. This includes computer products, such as computer chips. About 15,000 Vermont workers—almost one third of the state's manufacturing workforce—are employed in this area. Most of the state's electrical machinery and

Vermont's largest manufacturing industry is the production of electrical components, such as those used in computers. This tiny computer chip lying on a keyboard has been magnified many times.

above. This technician is assembling a computer at IBM.

below. Marble is mined in Vermont's Green Mountains. Marble has commercial and artistic uses. This man is sculpting a figure from a block of marble at the Vermont Marble Company.

equipment is made in Burlington and its surrounding cities. Other items made in Vermont that are part of this category range from semiconductors to batteries.

Another important area of manufacturing in Vermont is nonelectric machinery, such as machine tools. About four thousand of the state's manufacturing workers are employed in this industry. Springfield, in the southeastern part of the state, is one of the state's main centers of machine-tool manufacturing.

There are also many smaller manufacturing industries that help keep Vermont running. Most of these industries make products from resources found in the state, such as wood and stone. Paper, furniture, and even hockey sticks are some of the many wood products made in Vermont. Products manufactured from stone include headstones and monuments. Other manufacturing companies make products out of metal—from ski poles to hardware to weapons.

Most of Vermont's workers are employed in service industries. Service industry workers serve people rather than make products. These workers may be doctors, gas station attendants, and bank tellers. In all, about two hundred thousand of Vermont's workers are employed in service industries.

One large category of services in Vermont includes finance, insurance, and real estate. Real estate agents make up the largest group of these service workers. Most of their earnings come from vacation homes that tourists buy or rent. Stockbrokers and bankers are also an important part of this category. About 12,000 Vermont citizens work in finance, insurance, and real estate. Most are employed in Burlington, the state's largest city.

The largest category of service industries in Vermont is community, social, and personal services. This category not only brings in the most money of all service industries, it is also first in terms of employ-ment. Almost seventy thousand people work in this area of services. These workers include nurses, mechanics, hotel clerks, and lawyers.

The third most important category of services in Vermont is wholesale and retail trade. Wholesale trade mainly involves selling goods in large amounts, usually to companies and stores. Retail trade involves selling smaller quantities of goods, usually to individuals. The state's largest areas of retail trade include restaurants, grocery stores, clothing stores, and car dealerships. In all, wholesale and retail trade employ about sixty thou-sand people, who help bring about two billion dollars into the state each year.

Vermont's tourist industry involves workers from almost all of the service categories. Summer and winter resorts employ ski instructors, reservation clerks, restaurant servers, and lift operators. Government service workers staff tourist information centers, public parks, and forests. Retail trade workers, such as gift-shop clerks and ski outfitters, also profit from the state's tourist industry. In all, Vermont's tourists bring in over $2 billion each year.

The tourist industry has thrived in Vermont for

Skiers from around the world come to Stowe to ski Vermont's highest mountain, Mount Mansfield.

Cross-country skiing is another one of Vermont's popular tourist activities.

almost 150 years now. However, agriculture is the oldest industry in the state, begun in the days of the Native Americans. Although agriculture has diminished in economic importance since the 1950s, the state's nearly 6,000 farms produce about $1.2 billion worth of farm products each year.

Most of Vermont's farmers are dairy farmers, and milk is the state's most important farm product. Cheese, ice cream, yogurt, and butter are other dairy products made in Vermont. In all, Vermont's dairy farms sell almost $37 million worth of products each year.

But milk is far from the only agricultural product produced in Vermont. Farmers also raise sheep, horses, and cattle. Potatoes, corn, and hay are some of the state's vegetable and grain crops. Apples are the main fruit grown in the state. Vermont also leads the nation in production of maple syrup, making almost four hundred thousand gallons each year.

Mining of mineral resources is another small but important area of Vermont's economy. Granite and marble are the two most important products mined in

Most people think of skiing when they think of Vermont tourism, but the state also has many vacationers in the summer.

the state, although limestone, slate, and talc are also important. Some of the world's largest granite quarries are found in and around Barre. Thousands of tons of marble are mined in Proctor each year. Only about six hundred of the state's workers are miners, but they still manage to bring in $65 million to the state each year.

Most Vermonters do not live in urban areas, but the state has still managed to keep a solid manufacturing base. Vermont's main products—milk and computer products—couldn't be more different. But they do have one thing in common. They're the ingredients to one of the nation's healthiest economies.

Apples are Vermont's major fruit crop.

Vermont's maple syrup is used to make candy, sugar, and even some soft drinks.

Ice Cream's Dream Team

Imagine you are going to start your own business. Who would you choose for your partner? How about your best friend? What would you make and sell? How about something you really enjoy, such as ice cream? Where would you like the business to be located? How about a small town with beautiful scenery and friendly people? Sounds pretty good so far. Now imagine your business is easy to learn and makes a lot of money quickly.

This may sound like an impossible dream, but Ben Cohen and Jerry Greenfield made this dream come true. They joined together to create Ben & Jerry's Homemade, Inc., an ice cream company in Vermont.

Ben and Jerry were both born in Brooklyn, New York, in 1951. They met and became friends in the seventh grade. After high school, Jerry, a National Merit Scholarship winner, went off to college in Ohio, hoping to become a doctor. While at school, he worked part-time as an ice cream scooper in the college cafeteria.

Ben went to college, too, but quit after a year and a half. He went back

Still going strong today, Ben Cohen (left) and Jerry Greenfield have turned an initial investment of $12,000 into a multimillion-dollar ice cream business.

to the job he had in high school, selling ice cream pops to neighborhood children from an ice cream van. Later, Ben returned to college again, studying pottery and jewelry making. He moved to New York City and worked many odd jobs while continuing his studies.

Meanwhile, Jerry finished college, but didn't go to a medical school. Instead, he moved to New York City,

worked as a lab technician, and shared an apartment with his old buddy, Ben.

In 1974 Ben moved to New York's Adirondack Mountains area to teach school. Jerry headed to North Carolina.

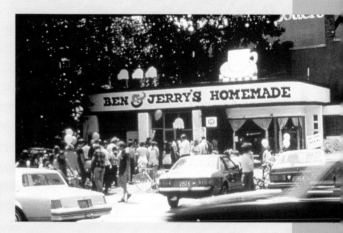

Ben & Jerry's first ice cream store was located in a former gas station.

Pint-size containers of ice cream roll off the production line at Ben & Jerry's Waterbury plant. All employees of Ben & Jerry's are allowed to take home three free pints of ice cream a day.

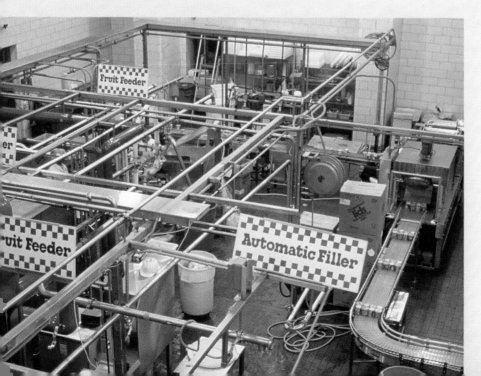

At Ben & Jerry's annual One World, One Heart Festival, festival goers write a brief message to Congress on a postcard and hand it in fo free ice cream. One World, One Heart sends thousands of postcards to Congres every year.

Neither of the friends was really satisfied with where his life was headed.

Ben and Jerry decided to start a food business together. They weren't sure what kind of business they wanted. They only knew that it had to be in a college town in the country and that it had to be something fun! After considering the options, they settled on making ice cream.

The two signed up to take a course in ice cream making by mail. Both friends got perfect scores on their final exams. It was time to start their business!

On May 5, 1978, with $12,000, they opened their first ice cream shop in Burlington, near the University of Vermont. At times they sold as many as 12 flavors. Jerry mixed the ice cream and Ben tasted it. They liked ice cream with chunks in it—things like candy bars and cookies—so that's what they made. Not every batch of ice cream turned out perfectly, but if it tasted good to Ben, they sold it. Soon their shop was popular in Burlington.

At first they were the only employees. Jerry made all the ice cream, and Ben tasted it, drove the truck, and ran the business. Soon they had people working for them. By 1980 the company was so successful that they had to hire more employees and move to a bigger space. They began selling their ice cream in pints with their pictures on the cartons to restaurants and grocery stores. The next year they had to move to an even bigger space. And then they opened another store. Ben & Jerry's ice cream really took off.

In 1984 they sold more than four million dollars worth of ice cream! But there was a problem. Ben and Jerry felt their business was becoming less fun. They were beginning to lose their personal touch with their customers and their workers. The partners thought of selling the company.

Instead of selling, however, Ben and Jerry made some big changes. If they could use the business to help other people and the environment, the company would still be fun. In 1985 they established the Ben & Jerry's Foundation. The foundation appoints 7.5 percent of the company's profits to good causes and community projects. The foundation is funded through the sales of all Ben and Jerry products. Some ice cream flavors are created to help certain groups of people. For example, the brownies in Chocolate Fudge Brownie are baked in Yonkers, New York, by formerly disadvantaged people in order to learn job skills. The coffee flavorings for Ben & Jerry's

coffee ice cream are purchased directly from small coffee growers in Mexico instead of from large companies. This puts more money directly into the hands of the small farmers.

Did giving so much money away cause the company to go broke? No! In 1997 Ben & Jerry's sold almost $174 million worth of ice cream. Over two hundred thousand people a year tour the Ben & Jerry's manufacturing plant in Waterbury, making it one of the most popular tourist attractions in Vermont.

Obviously, people care about Ben & Jerry's. Maybe that's because Ben and Jerry care about people. Maybe it's because Ben and Jerry, the company they run, and the people who work for them still know how to have fun!

Looking at these ice cream bars, it's easy to believe that the way to the world's heart is through its stomach.

Vermont's Simple Inspiration

Perhaps not surprisingly, much of the culture of Vermont speaks of its lush rural landscape with a quiet, yet powerful beauty. Perhaps the best example of this simple but rich culture can be found in the works of Vermont's most famous poet, Robert Frost.

Robert Frost was born in San Francisco, but he moved to New England at age ten and remained there for the rest of his life. Almost all of his poetry speaks about life in New England. He incorporated scenes and images from its landscapes as well as the natural speech patterns of its people. Frost remains one of America's most popular poets, but he had trouble publishing his work in America at the beginning of his career. He had to publish his first book, *A Boy's Will*, in Great Britain when no American publishers would accept it. Once the British critics began to rave about Frost's work, American publishers realized the mistake they had made in passing him up. His first two books were accepted by a New York publisher in 1915, two years after their publication in Great Britain.

This sculpture, "Whale Tails," is in the Vermont town of Randolph Center.

Frost spent much of his life in New Hampshire but at last settled in Vermont beginning in 1920. Among the many honors he received during his lifetime are four Pulitzer Prizes in poetry and a gold medal of honor from Congress. Vermont made him Poet Laureate of the state in 1961. Citizens of Vermont proudly cite Frost's assessment of their state as one of the two best in the nation—an honor they share with neighboring New Hampshire.

Another Vermont writer proved himself a literary leader almost two hundred years earlier than Frost. Playwright Royall Tyler was born in Boston in 1757 but moved to Vermont around age thirty. He remained

Vermont contains more than one hundred covered bridges. Middlebury's Pulp Mill Bridge is the oldest covered bridge in the state.

there the rest of his life. Tyler wrote America's first theatrical comedy, *The Contrast*, which debuted in New York City in 1787. Tyler incorporated the flavor of New England into his "Yankee" characters.

Born almost a century after Tyler, Dorothy Canfield Fisher became another of Vermont's major literary figures. Like Tyler, Fisher moved to Vermont around age thirty. She was originally from Kansas. Her best work came from her years spent in Arlington, Vermont. She wrote many books for adults, but is better known for her children's books. Countless children today still enjoy her book *Understood Betsy*, first published in 1917.

Yet another cultural figure born elsewhere but drawn to Vermont's beauty and simplicity was artist Norman Rockwell. Rockwell settled in Arlington, Vermont, for about 15 years. He often used Vermont residents as models for his drawings and paintings. He specialized in portraying everyday life in mid-twentieth-century New England. President Gerald Ford awarded Rockwell the Presidential Medal of Freedom in 1977 for his lifetime of dedicated work. Since Rockwell's death in 1978, Vermont citizens have established two museums in his honor. The Norman Rockwell Exhibit in Arlington and the Norman Rockwell Museum in Rutland hold many of his best works.

Vermont artist William Morris Hunt painted American landscapes a century earlier than Rockwell. Born in Brattleboro in 1824, Hunt began his artistic career in Paris and brought the Romantic styles of the time back to the States. Hunt is best known for his

Autumn foliage at Green Mountain National Forest and across the state is renowned for its beauty.

Almost every town in Vermont has at least one craft shop, with handmade items such as artistic glassware displayed in its window.

portraits and his murals in the capitol building of New York in Albany. The Vermont landscapes he painted later in life, however, are the paintings Vermont residents find closest to their hearts.

Richard Morris Hunt, William's younger brother, became a famous architect. Richard Hunt also studied in Paris, where he helped design many buildings. Hunt is noted for his versatility—his designs include luxury homes and even the base of the Statue of Liberty. Hunt also helped found the American Institute of Architects and served as the organization's president from 1888 until his retirement.

A Vermont sculptor of the same era as the Hunts was Hiram Powers. Born in 1805 in Woodstock, Powers became one of the most popular sculptors of his time when his statue "Greek Slave" was first shown in 1843. Two of his most famous sculptures are of Benjamin Franklin and Thomas Jefferson. Both of these sculptures are housed in the Capitol building in Washington, D.C.

As proud as Vermont is of its famous artists, it also prizes its lesser-known but equally talented folk artists. Handmade tools, clothing, quilts, baskets, and other traditional crafts are highly valued for their beauty and simplicity of design. Such museums as Middlebury's Sheldon Museum and the Vermont State Craft Center at Frog Hollow display all types of this country art. Craft shows across the state, such as Northfield's Vermont Quilt Festival and Stowe's Foliage Craft Fair, also celebrate the type of art from which Vermont's culture was built.

Vermont also strongly supports the performing arts. The Vermont Symphony Orchestra was founded in 1934. In the summer, Vermont is brimming with theater and music, including the Marlboro Music Festival and the Vermont Mozart Festival.

Many artists have come to Vermont to write, paint, and sculpt in peace and quiet. It's more than peace and quiet that keeps them in the state, however. The beauty and simplicity of the Vermont landscape provide an ingredient even more necessary to the life of an artist—inspiration.

Hiram Powers sculpted this statue of Benjamin Franklin in 1862.

Backwoods Bach

Blanche Moyse grew up in Switzerland and moved to Marlboro, Vermont in 1949. In Switzerland and across Europe, Moyse was a highly successful violinist. Her most distinguished prize was a first-place ranking from the Geneva Conservatory of Music. But Blanche Moyse wanted to do more than win praise and prizes. She also wanted to inspire young musicians to reach the heights of their talent. She started by establishing a music department at Marlboro College in Vermont. Her musical accomplishments since then are amazing.

Back in 1949 Moyse was told that starting a music department at Marlboro would be "pioneer work." But she didn't realize just how difficult pioneer work could be. "Had we not been Europeans, had we been Americans instead," she remembers, "we would have known what 'pioneer work' meant. It might have frightened us. But we didn't know."

After Moyse had her music department running, she spread her music to the rest of the community, helping to organize the Marlboro Music Festival. But the community wasn't sure yet whether or not they wanted an annual festival of classical music.

It took some time, but Blanche Moyse gained the trust of the people of southern Vermont—and that

The countryside of Vermont, says Blanche Moyse, is "part of my life, the same as music."

trust led to undying support. They have since helped her establish the Brattleboro Music Center, the New England Bach Festival, and the Blanche Moyse Chorale. At age 89, Moyse's rigorous standards have not slackened. Her groups continue to win enthusiastic acclaim across the nation, along with concert dates at such famous sites as Boston's Emmanuel Church and New York's Carnegie Hall.

Blanche Moyse loves her music, and she has grown to love Vermont just as much. "This beauty goes to my heart," she says. "I mean, there is not

Part of Blanche Moyse's secret to success is her personal commitment to her musicians. Some of the singers in her chorale have been performing with her since the 1950s.

"I don't consider myself a leader," says Blanche Moyse. "I consider myself a teacher and, in the end, an inspirer also, having a vision."

one day which is not beautiful. Every day is different. There's not one that repeats the other. And that gives an incredible image of continuous creation."

Vermont has contributed even more than the countryside to Moyse's love of the state. "The people are friendly and warm. [They] make an effort to contribute, to create something great and wonderful." But the people of southern Vermont know that they can't take much of the credit. It's Blanche Moyse who has brought them the "great and wonderful" gift of music—a gift that they plan to keep and nurture for many more years.

Town Meeting

There's something special that happens in Vermont every spring. On the first Tuesday in March, the people in each of the state's nearly 250 towns come together for town meetings. Town Meeting Day is a state holiday. Schools, banks, and other public institutions are closed. Everybody gathers at the town hall to discuss and vote upon their town's budget, their local officials, and other issues. Any adult citizen of the town has the right to add to the debate.

While few Vermont citizens miss this opportunity to have their votes counted and their voices heard, the nation's voting record tells a different story. Across the nation, political scientists are lamenting a drop in voter turnout. Many blame this depressing trend on an increasingly lazy population. But University of Vermont professor Frank Bryan thinks that it's the nation's system of voting, not the voters, that is to blame. As Bryan explains, "People ask me . . . why is it that people don't vote as much as they used to? And I think it's because people don't see the connection between voting and public policy. . . . They don't see any reason to go vote because they're not sure it's going to change anything."

Towns take special care to make sure that their yearly meetings are accessible to everyone.

This photo shows a town meeting in Cabot, Vermont. Vermont has been holding town meetings for two hundred years.

Citizens of Vermont, however, gather every year to witness their votes being counted. The issues voted upon at town meetings range from road maintenance, to the upkeep of the Fire Department, to the support of arts councils and community service bureaus. The amount of money allocated to these budget items ranges from $50 to $500,000. They also meet the people that they vote into—or out of—office. They realize how much difference one vote can make.

"In a town meeting," says Bryan, "when you go into that meeting hall and vote someone out of office . . .

you can't escape it. You've got to see them. You've got to eat lunch with them after you voted them out of office in the town hall. That's human-scale politics. And that's the beauty of the town meeting. It forces us to be responsible for our actions immediately." The most important aspect of Vermont's "human-scale" politics is its requirement that every citizen think carefully about everyone involved before casting a vote. Town meetings are a serious responsibility and a unique privilege that few Vermont citizens—if any at all—want to trade.

Slowly but Steadily Ahead

As states across the nation are becoming more urban and more crowded, Vermont is one of the few places left to escape the crowds. In area it's the third largest state in New England, but it has maintained the nation's third-smallest population. As more and more people discover the beauty and solitude of the Green Mountain State, however, it becomes harder and harder to keep that beauty from becoming spoiled.

The state legislature first began to address this issue when it passed the Environmental Control Law in 1970. In 1988 Vermont legislated the Growth Management Act to monitor development in the state even more closely. In recent years, however, these laws have been challenged. Some people feel Vermont is being left behind in terms of progress and economic development. They believe that if some of these environmental laws aren't relaxed, then high technology—and the lifestyles of the future—will bypass Vermont altogether.

The rapid progress of the twentieth century has not greatly altered Vermont's natural landscape. However, the coming century will challenge Vermont's environmental limits.

Two-thirds of the people of Vermont live in non-urban areas, making Vermont the most rural state in the nation.

There are many benefits to keeping Vermont's development gradual, however. Vermont has been ranked as one of the safest states in the nation. Burlington has been repeatedly voted one of the best places to raise a family. In addition, development may destroy Vermont's rural settings, prompting many of its eight million yearly visitors to look for somewhere else to find peace and quiet. That might end up being more harmful to the state's economy than keeping a tight rein on development.

Vermont's sparse population also seems to have improved its quality of education. Because schools are less crowded, teachers and administrators have more time to concentrate on the development of individual students. In addition, some of the state's educational programs have won respect nationwide.

In many ways Vermont is like old, wooden furniture, glowing softly from years of care and shaped by years of use. Creating the future here means polishing what has proven itself over centuries. Vermont residents who want to speed up development in the state seem ready to throw away that piece of furniture and start from scratch. So far, the people of Vermont continue to support a steady pace of development, thus assuring the unique character of the Green Mountain State for years to come.

Important Historical Events

1500s   Algonquin Native Americans war with the Iroquois for control of what is now Vermont.

1609   Samuel de Champlain explores the area, claims it for France, and names Lake Champlain. His party later helps the Algonquins against the Iroquois.

1724   Fort Dummer is established. The Dutch found a community at Pownal.

1749   The New Hampshire governor begins selling plots of land in Vermont called the New Hampshire Grants.

1763   The French and Indian War ends. Great Britain gains control of Vermont.

1764   Great Britain backs New York's claims to the Vermont area.

1770   The Green Mountain Boys organize to defend their land against "Yorkers."

1775   The Revolutionary War begins in April. Ethan Allen and the Green Mountain Boys capture Fort Ticonderoga from the British in May.

1777   Vermont declares itself an independent republic.

1783   The Revolutionary War ends, and the United States wins its independence from Great Britain.

1790   Vermont pays New York thirty thousand dollars to give up its land claims to the area.

1791   Vermont becomes the fourteenth state.

1812   The War of 1812 begins, damaging the state's economy.

1823   Alexander Twilight graduates from Middlebury College.

1865   Dairy products and mining dominate Vermont's economy.

1881   Vermont-born Chester A. Arthur becomes the twenty-first President of the United States.

1891   Vermont becomes the first state with an office of publicity to encourage tourism.

1917   The United States enters World War I. Vermont donates one million dollars and sends twenty thousand soldiers.

1923   Vermont-born Calvin Coolidge becomes the thirtieth President of the United States.

1927   The Winooski and Connecticut rivers flood, killing about sixty people.

1930   Thousands of Vermont citizens are out of work as the Great Depression takes hold of the country.

1934   The Vermont Symphony Orchestra is founded.

1949   The Vermont Development Department is established.

1961   Robert Frost becomes Poet Laureate of Vermont.

1970   Vermont passes the Environmental Control Law.

1978   The first Ben & Jerry's ice cream store opens in Burlington.

1984   Madeleine Kunin is the first woman elected governor of Vermont.

1988   Vermont passes the Growth Management Act to monitor the use of land in the state.

1991   Vermont celebrates its two hundredth birthday.

1994   Vermont is ranked the safest state in the nation.

45

Vermont's flag features the state coat of arms on a blue background. Two pine branches, along with the state name and motto printed on a red ribbon, border the lower part of the shield. The head of a stag sits above the shield. Inside a gold ornate border, the shield depicts a cow and three sheaves of grain beneath a pine tree, which symbolize agriculture.

Vermont Almanac

Nickname. The Green Mountain State

Capital. Montpelier

State Bird. Hermit thrush

State Flower. Red clover

State Tree. Sugar maple

State Motto. Freedom and Unity

State Song. "Hail, Vermont!"

State Abbreviations. Vt. (traditional); VT (postal)

Statehood. March 4, 1791, the 14th state

Government. Congress: U.S. senators, 2; U.S. representatives, 1. State Legislature: senators, 30; representatives, 150. Counties: 14

Area. 9,615 sq mi (24,903 sq km), 43rd in size among the states

Greatest Distances. north/south, 158 mi (255 km); east/west, 97 mi (156 km)

Elevation. Highest: Mount Mansfield, 4,393 ft (1,339 m). Lowest: Lake Champlain, 95 ft (29 m)

Population. 1990 Census: 564,964 (10% increase over 1980), 48th in size among the states. Density: 59 persons per sq mi (23 persons per sq km). Distribution: 32% urban, 68% rural. 1980 Census: 511,456

Economy. *Agriculture*: dairy products, maple syrup, apples, potatoes, corn, hay, beef cattle, sheep, horses, eggs. *Manufacturing*: electrical machinery and equipment, nonelectrical machinery, paper and wood products. *Mining*: granite, marble, limestone, slate, talc

State Seal

State Bird: Hermit thrush

State Flower: Red clover

Annual Events

- ★ Winter Carnival in Stowe (January)
- ★ Town Meeting Day, statewide (March)
- ★ Vermont Maple Festival in St. Albans (April)
- ★ Ben & Jerry's One World One Heart Festival in Warren (June)
- ★ Discover Jazz Festival in Burlington (June)
- ★ Fiddler's Contest in Hardwick (July)
- ★ Vermont Quilt Festival in Northfield (July)
- ★ Hildene Crafts Fair in Manchester (August)
- ★ Champlain Valley Exposition in Essex Junction (August/September)
- ★ State Fair in Rutland (September)
- ★ Foliage Festivals, statewide (September/October)

Places to Visit

- ★ Ben & Jerry's Ice Cream Factory in Waterbury
- ★ Bennington Battle Monument in Bennington
- ★ Lake Champlain Basin Science Center in Burlington
- ★ Green Mountain National Forest
- ★ Hyde Log Cabin in Grand Isle
- ★ Maple Grove Maple Museum in St. Johnsbury
- ★ Robert Frost Recreation Trail in Ripton
- ★ Shelburne Museum in Shelburne
- ★ Stellafane Observatory in Springfield
- ★ Vermont Institute of Natural Science and Vermont Raptor Center in Woodstock

Index